I0840086

CUBAN RAFTERS

CUBAN RAFTERS

Cármen Vázquez-Fernández

Collection NARRATIVE

Front Page: Casa del Balsero (Cayo Hueso, Florida).

Cover photo and interiors of the author.

I dedicate this book to my Cuban brothers who tried to flee Cuba and lost their lives in the Straits of Florida since 1959.

To the memory of the children, women, and men—all Cubans—who perished in the sinking of the tugboat "March 13," perpetrated by Cuban coastguards on the fateful day of July 13, 1994.

In memory of the Cuban pilots of "Hermanos al Rescate," whose civilian planes were shot down by military aircraft of the Cuban government on February 24, 1996.

As a tribute to all the victims of Castroism, and to their families who still mourn their deaths, I denounce the dictatorial regime of Fidel Castro. I know firsthand what it means to be a Cuban rafter.

This book is also dedicated to my son, Vincent Fernandez, born in Newark, New Jersey, USA, under a sky and a land of freedom.

THE AUTHOR

Foreword

This is a testimonial book, a denunciation, and it is written in a straightforward and accessible manner so that readers can fully grasp the tragedy of the Cuban rafters.

I was born in Havana in 1969, ten years after the Cuban Revolution. In Cuba, I knew only the regime established in 1959 until I managed to escape the island in 1991, like countless other Cuban rafters. For twenty-two years, I lived under an unyielding dictatorship, and I can testify to the crimes of this totalitarian regime that masquerades as a revolution.

This chronicle of the Cuban rafters is based on real events and stems from my need to expose to the world the sole person responsible for this human tragedy: the dictator Fidel Castro.

As a believer in God, I can tell the tyrant that he may find salvation in this life, but his soul will find no peace after death. He will be haunted by thousands of restless souls seeking justice. These are words I have kept silent for a long time. I admit my fear—a terrible and paralyzing fear that forced me, like my fellow citizens, to wear a mask. Living in a totalitarian dictatorship like Cuba's breeds that fear and silence, which are pure acts of survival.

With the Cuban Revolution in the early 1960s, Cubans lost all liberties and rights. Since then, we have endured ideological shifts and the whims of a tyrant. All dissent, disagreement, or opposition was systematically punished with long years of political imprisonment, execution, or bitter exile.

The massive exodus of rafters signifies another outrage against the Cuban people by the Castro dictatorship. We must be incredibly desperate and without prospects to risk our lives and those of our families in a perilous journey of 90 nautical miles. Many failed, either arrested or killed by Cuban authorities or drowned in the deadly Straits of Florida.

Cuban rafters are synonymous with lovers of freedom. For this word, we risk the most precious thing—our lives and those of our loved ones.

When I arrived in the United States of America, I set foot for the first time in a land of freedom and opportunity. It was a leap into the unknown, a sudden transformation of my life. I didn't even know what Christmas was. I grew up without it, knowing it was celebrated elsewhere but not understanding its meaning. Castro sought to make Cuba an atheist state. It was frowned upon to

attend church if you wanted to study or work. The question was always asked at school enrollment: "Do you have a religion?" The answer was invariably, "No." I was baptized at 22 years old in the USA. I had to go far to be baptized properly! But now I am free, even though I live in exile, far from my mother and the rest of my family.

Because I know the tyrant and have suffered his abuses firsthand, I want the world to know him too: This is the true face of the dictator Fidel Castro! Here are his crimes against humanity: directly responsible for the sinking of the tugboat "March 13" and the shooting down of the "Brothers to the Rescue" planes. This is why I wrote these pages. I hope this book makes the world reflect and learn more about the Cuban people's tragedy: the truth about Cubans and the lie of Castro.

Cuban rafters is a story, but it is only a grain of sand compared to the atrocities and murders committed by the old, gray-haired dictator against my people over these disastrous forty years, which have remained unpunished. How much longer?

CHAPTER I:
CUBA

Havana

floridita
LA CUNA DEL DAIQUIRI
ENTRE LOS 7 BA
MÁS FAMOSOS DEL M

I will tell you a story that I do not know how to narrate. How can I describe so much pain? How do you explain the frustration of an entire Island or the despair of a generation that grew up with the Revolution?

On that morning of May '91, a strong breeze swept through Havana. It was said that a cold front was coming. There were four people on Havana's Malecon: three boys and one girl, speaking in hushed tones.

"Tomorrow is the day. Fidel just finished his speech for May Day and pulled all the surveillance off the streets," said Carlos. He was about 26 years old, and his words were confident and steady, reflecting his own demeanor. The others were Ana, 21, Eddy, around 20, and Lazaro, 35

"Hey... tell me, chico, at five in the morning, the president of the Committee* was banging on all the doors. It seemed like he was going to knock them down, forcing people to go to the Plaza de la Revolution. I didn't even bother to answer, and neither did many others," said Eddy.

"Oh Eddy, you weren't the only one. They knocked on my door too, and I didn't answer. They said, 'come out, our commander Fidel speaks today.' He means their president, but not my president. I didn't even pay attention.

These communists are crazy. I don't know what they defend or where they are going. Look at us, we're their products, and they claim we're all for their Revolution," Ana said, while everyone kept their gazes fixed on the sea.

"Well, let's get to the reason we're here. Everything is ready: water and oil are already on the raft," said Lazaro.

"Yes, Lazaro, but you're forgetting the most important thing: today we have to say goodbye to our families, and that's hard," Ana replied.

"Ana, we know this, but you have to be very discreet. We all agreed on this—

complete discretion. This could cost us dearly; we all understand that, right?" Carlos emphasized.

"But don't worry, Lazaro, we're not going to give the communists the satisfaction of catching us. From Miami, I'm going to send a postcard that says: 'Look, guys, this is freedom,'" Carlos commented.

They all smiled, and Ana, addressing Carlos, said, "Well, can you tell me what we're going to do about this bad weather? We can't calm the sea."

"I'll tell you something: everything is already on the raft. If we're caught with water and oil on the raft without having left, we're all prisoners. So, we must leave tomorrow. We don't have any more time, and may God protect us."

"Just in case, yesterday we went to the corner to see San Lazaro," Lazaro added.

The four remained silent, perhaps because everything had been said. Then went their separate ways, leaving only Carlos and

Ana together. They were husband and wife, and they had a little girl whom they would leave in the care of her grandmother. As they walked, they talked...

"I'm very nervous, Carlos. The baby is only four years old. It's too risky to take her on this trip—the worst could happen. I know my mom isn't in the best condition to take care of her until we can bring her with us legally, but the thought of being away from her is killing me," Ana said.

"You know that every time our baby accompanies us to find the place where I plan to pick you up on the coast, she gets very sick—damn asthma, Chica, you know it. And you know we've tried, but it's impossible. If we don't go now, we'll keep living in oppression, and she'll grow up the same way. Maybe one day she would condemn us.

for not having taken her out of this. But I'm not going to risk her life. She's innocent, and she's not asking to leave. A trip like this, with her asthma, could cost her life," Carlos replied.

They walked several blocks, from Havana's Malecon to Ana's mother's house, where their daughter was staying. They stopped at the entrance of the building, which was in very bad condition, perhaps due to age or lack of maintenance.

Some timbers held it up to prevent collapse, but people still lived there. It was all they had, the little that was left to them.

"Hi, Mommy," Ana said to her mom.

"Mommy…"

A cute little girl with big eyes and long, curly hair appeared and hugged her mother. Hugging made her both totally happy, but the pain and anguish grew in Ana.

"Mami, we have to talk. Tomorrow is the day, and if God wills, everything will be fine. Yesterday we went to the church in Rincon. What I want most is for you to take care of my daughter and to take good care of yourself," Ana said.

And she approached her mother and hugged her tightly, as if wanting to take them with her. "Mami, I am very nervous, but I know this is the best. I want to be free. I'm sick of this oppression. We grew up with the Revolution, but we must not be blind to see that everything is a fraud. We are living it, so we know it.

When the Soviet Union realized that Communism was obsolete and made changes, I thought it was cool. They stopped being communists! Not like here, where this government doesn't let people think. There are no elections, nothing. When the Soviet Union collapsed, they collected all the Soviet magazines, and Fidel said that if they were tearing down Lenin's statues, we were going to build them here. He claimed it wasn't communism imposed on us, only socialism! And he doesn't even believe it."

"Oh, my daughter, I don't know anymore. This can cost you your life, and your little girl needs you."

"Mommy, it will be a matter of little time. As soon as I get the American residency, I'll bring her over. Maybe within a year.

You know we're going to get it right; otherwise, we wouldn't be doing this."

"Even now, everything seems like a dream. I think this is not true and that it's not happening to me..."

Her mother broke into sobs. Ana hugged her and began to cry too.

"Mami, the baby is in the room and can hear us. Please, don't make it harder..."

"No, mi hija, I'm fine. Don't worry. I got you the little tank you asked for. Take care of yourself, girl. Look what happened to your brother Tony, who tried to leave, built the raft with his own

hands, and they didn't let him put it in the water. It cost him a year in prison, and they treated him like a criminal. Such a healthy boy. Don't you think you're a little exhausted with all this mess?"

"Yes, Mommy, I know what Tony went through. But these communists aren't going to catch us. He was tricked into leaving the country by a secret agent who worked for Security and later denounced him. That dog probably got a medal, but that's what the Communists are...

Do you remember when they detained him for a whole month in Villa Maritima, and every time we went to see him, that little captain said?

Tony wouldn't be released until he accepted the Revolution because he had made a mistake?" "How can I not remember? Those were days of much suffering, and every time we visited him, your brother only repeated that he wasn't with the Revolution, that he didn't believe in it, and that when he left, he would try to leave illegally again."

"And you remember, Mami, that day they called us from Villa Maritima, saying they had to take Tony to the hospital because he had gotten sick? When we saw him, his arms were black with punctures from the injections. After that, he said, 'I'm sorry, I was wrong. When I get out,

I'll work for this.' But he never raised his face or looked us in the eyes. They had broken him.

They made him humiliate himself at 22 years old. But when we visited him in Combinado del Este, he didn't think so.

He only told us he needed time to get out of there."

"Well, Ana, it's about time. I can't say goodbye..."

"Carlos, wait for me..."

"It seems he prefers it this way, Mommy. No parting. I must go. I will take you with me always."

Ana hugged her daughter and mother as hard as she could, with much love and despair, and ran through the streets of her hometown as fast as her legs allowed, never to return.

CHAPTER II:
A RAFTER'S STORY

Rafters at sea....

As night fell, they all gathered at Carlos's house. Silence filled the room; they exchanged glances without speaking, waiting for the departure time. Some smoked and reminisced about their loved ones, but their minds were occupied with the possibility of being caught by the army on the coast or by the Cuban coastguards at sea. This was not their only concern.

The sea was another formidable threat. They were aware of the impending bad weather, but their departure date and time were set, like an unchangeable plane ticket.

Their course was northward with a slight deviation to the east. This was all they knew. They had no fixed destination and weren't even sure it was the right direction to Florida, but it was the only information they had.

They placed their faith in God and la Virgen del Cobre, believing they would not be abandoned. They also hoped the sea would calm and allow them to reach freedom alive.

The day ended, and dawn broke on May 2, 1991. At Carlos's house, Radio Martí played: "Now we will give you the weather."

"Ana, we have to leave. We know there's a storm at sea. Radio Martí has repeated it again and again, 'Do not go to the sea today, it is dangerous with the bad weather,' but there's nothing left to do. Carlos and Lazaro left at two in the morning, and it's five now. We must go," Eddy said.

"Yes, I know. Let's go now. I think it's better not to keep thinking and thinking," Ana answered.

They left quickly but tried not to make any noise. They took the bus to the designated departure point on the coast of Boca de Jaruco in Havana. The trip was silent. Eddy and Ana were lost in their thoughts, silently saying goodbye to everything and everyone.

"Eddy, this is the stop."

"Hurry up, Chica. Driver, a moment, please, driver..."

They got off the bus and walked to the coast. In front of them lay the sea, and with it, their fear of departure or death.
"Hey, Ana, look, there goes the raft. It's them," Eddy said.

"It's okay. Now we must wait and stay as we are," Ana replied as she helped him pull out a few spools of fishing line. They took their hooks and sat on the rocks to fish and wait. Time seemed infinite. They had arrived at dawn, and now it was nearing noon.

"This is taking forever. Those two fishermen who were here when we arrived don't seem to be leaving. Carlos can't pick us up if there are people on the coast who can see us," Eddy remarked.

"Look, Carlos is coming toward us. What do we do?" Ana asked.

"I'd say stay quiet," Eddy suggested.

By noon, the sky was gray, and a light drizzle began to fall. A boat about twenty feet long, named Ailema, with colors matching the Cuban flag—white, blue, and red—cut through the waves heading straight for the coast.

"Jump," Eddy said.

He took Ana by the arm and helped her jump, giving her a boost from the rocky coast into the boat, then followed her aboard. It all happened within minutes. Carlos reversed the boat and then steered north.

"We made it... soon we will be free," one of them said.

They had sailed about two miles when Ana, who was lying on the floor of the boat to avoid being seen, shouted, "Oh, my God, a helicopter is flying above us!"

Carlos quickly grabbed a tarp from the boat and threw it over Ana and Eddy.

"Everything will be fine," he reassured them. "Lazaro and I have permission to go fishing."

The helicopter flew over them, and they pretended to be fishing, continuing their journey.

Carlos was sitting at the back edge of the boat, gripping a large piece of wood that served as the rudder. He stayed in that position for hours, fighting against the worsening waves and bad weather to keep the boat from capsizing. The rain was relentless, and the sea's fury grew with each passing minute, battering the boat with wave after wave, leaving it filled with water.

Three hours later, or maybe more—time became irrelevant when survival was the only concern—Carlos's voice broke the tension.

"Ana, the Havana Lighthouse is no longer visible. We've passed the 18-mile mark. Come sit here by my side. I can't let go of the rudder, or we'll be turned around."

Ana tried to sit up, her body numb, and her clothes soaked from the waves. Her black hair was wet, and her brown eyes reflected despair. Minutes later, she began to vomit.

"Try to raise your head, Ana," Carlos urged.

"I can't, Carlos. I'm too dizzy. Everything moves too much. Give me something to cover my head so I can't see."

Carlos took the canvas and covered her as best he could. Movement was nearly impossible due to the heavy rain and waves; falling into the sea was a constant risk.

"Ana, how are you?" he called out.

"Alright," she replied weakly, though her sobs betrayed her struggle.

They endured busy hours, facing immense waves and a very dark night. The first night at sea awaited them, a night without a moon or stars...

"Well, gentlemen," Lazaro began, his voice trembling, "I've never seen anything like this in my life. It's pitch black out here—I can't even see my hands, let alone the sea or the sky."

"Hey, calm down, Lazaro," Carlos interjected. "This is serious. Look, the compass is spinning in all directions."

"Carlos, I hate to say this, but if I fall into the sea, they'll never find me. It's so dark, I can't see anything..."

"Listen, Lazaro, listen," Eddy chimed in. "We don't even have a compass."

"Maybe you're just not seeing it well in this darkness," Carlos suggested.

"No, the compass glows in the dark. It seems like we're passing through the infamous Bermuda Triangle. They say compasses go haywire here. Could it be true?"

Whether they were in the Bermuda Triangle or not, they preferred not to dwell on it any longer.

"Carlos, do you smell that burning smell, like burnt rubber?" Lazaro asked.

"Yeah, something's definitely burning. Quick, we need to check the engine."

Carlos sprang into action, inspecting the engine while battling the rolling waves.

"It's overheated," he declared. "If we don't shut it off now, it'll explode."

"What can we do?" Eddy asked.

"Someone needs to hold the rudder while I shut off the engine. With these waves and the engine off, we'll start turning."

Lazaro grabbed the long pole to keep the boat on course while Carlos shut off the engine. Together with Eddy, they tried to fix the engine, but it was too hot to restart.

"I can't get it to turn back on. We'll have to wait until it cools down," Carlos announced.

"Carlos, look, Ana's getting worse again," Eddy observed.

Ana had lost the will to fight. The relentless rocking of the boat intensified her dizziness, causing her to vomit repeatedly, though there was nothing left in her stomach. It was the hardest thing she had ever endured.

Carlos turned off the engine and lay down next to Ana, barely able to sit up. The others joined them on the floor of the boat, seeking shelter under the tarp from the pounding waves and rain.
All they could do now was wait, hoping for a miracle in the darkness of the night. It didn't take ten minutes before Carlos sprang into action.

"Get ready, this boat's turning!" he shouted, rushing to take control of the rudder. The other two men joined him, fear etched on their faces. Ana remained motionless, unsure of what to do or where to go in the vast ocean.

"I have an idea," Carlos declared. "If I tie this tarp to the mast, it'll act as a makeshift sail until we can get the engine running again."

"Wait, Carlos," Lazaro interjected, "Your plan's all well and good, but whoever goes up to the bow is as good as dead— drowned, disappeared, or shark bait. Count me out."

"I didn't say nobody's going up," Carlos retorted. "I'll do it. You two hold me tight, and I'll get it done."

With grim determination, Carlos climbed amid the raging waves while the others held on desperately.

The rain lashed down relentlessly, obscuring his view, but he managed to secure the tarp before descending.

"Help me down," Carlos called out as he returned to Ana's side.

"Would you like some water? How are you feeling?" he asked softly as he settled Ana back down.

Ana trembled, her face flushed with fever, but there was nothing to give her.

"Carlos..." she murmured weakly.

"Just hold on, things are getting rough," he reassured her. The boat leaned dangerously to one side, the waves threatening to capsize them. Carlos scrambled to the mast and swiftly untied the tarp, letting it fall to the deck.

"Help me here, I'm going to try starting the engine again," he instructed.

With a determined effort, Carlos managed to restart the engine and resumed his place at the rudder. The sun beat down mercilessly, the rain having ceased but the sea still roiling with immense waves.

"Carlos, this engine's running too hot. It smells like burnt rubber," Eddy warned.

"I didn't want to turn it off again for Ana's sake, but there's no other choice," Carlos replied solemnly.

Carlos made the decision to turn off the boat's engine once again, leaving them adrift with an uncertain direction.

About twenty minutes later...

"Look, a ship is coming toward us," someone exclaimed.

"It's a cargo ship, and it's huge," another confirmed.

They all watched anxiously as the massive vessel approached, waving their hands, and shouting for attention.

Carlos gently lifted Ana into his arms, trying to rouse her.

"We're saved, my love. Look over there," he exclaimed, pointing toward the approaching ship. "We can't just stay here and wait for them," Carlos observed, his tone serious.

"You're crazy, Carlos. This is our salvation. We must wait for them to pick us up," someone protested.

"No, if that ship comes to us with these waves, we'll collide with it. I haven't seen any signs that they're coming to rescue us.

We need to move now," Carlos insisted firmly.

Everyone rallied to help Carlos. He restarted the engine and set a course, uncertain of where it would lead them, but hopeful it wouldn't be back to Cuba. Eddy burst into laughter, his amusement echoing over the waves.

"Don't tell me you've lost your mind, Carlos," someone remarked.

"No, look, the compass is working, and we're heading north," Carlos replied, a mix of relief and grim determination evident on his face.

"Guiding Light"

As the storm finally subsides, the morning sun rises over the horizon, casting a soft, golden glow over the tranquil waters. The group of Cuban refugees aboard the small boat, their spirits weary and hearts heavy with uncertainty, find themselves surrounded by a newfound sense of calm after the chaos of the night.

As they navigate the choppy waters, their eyes are drawn to a pod of dolphins gracefully gliding through the sea. The dolphins, their sleek bodies glistening in the morning light, seem to dance and play around the boat, their movements fluid and captivating.

For Ana, who has been struggling with dizziness and nausea from the relentless storm, the sight of the dolphins brings a glimmer of hope and a moment of relief. She watches in awe as the dolphins leap out of the water, their playful chirps echoing across the sea.

Carlos, who has been steering the boat with unwavering determination, feels a surge of emotion as he watches the dolphins' graceful movements. In their playful antics, he sees a reflection of the resilience and spirit of freedom that has kept them going through the darkest of times.

As the dolphins continue to swim alongside the boat, their presence feels like a guiding light in the vast expanse of the sea. The refugees are filled with a sense of wonder and gratitude, finding solace in the beauty and freedom of these magnificent creatures.

In this moment, surrounded by the gentle companionship of the dolphins, the group finds a renewed sense of hope and unity.

They are reminded that even in the face of uncertainty and adversity, there are moments of beauty and grace that can light their way forward.

As the dolphins eventually swim off into the distance, the refugees are left with a profound sense of peace and determination. They know that they are not alone in their journey, and that if they hold onto hope and resilience, they can navigate the challenges that lie ahead.

This encounter with the dolphins becomes a symbol of hope and guidance for the group, a reminder that even in the darkest of times, there are moments of light and beauty that can sustain them on their path to freedom.

And so, the second day at sea came to an end. May 3 concluded without the hope of solid ground and freedom, but with a fervent desire to reach safety. The night descended once again, dark and foreboding, as Lazaro prepared to signal with a light. The waves remained relentless, seeming to dictate the small boat's journey.

"I see lights... Yes," Carlos announced.

"What are you talking about, Carlos? I don't see anything," Eddy replied skeptically.

"Don't listen to him, kid. I don't see a thing either," Lazaro chimed in, frustration evident in his voice.

And so, a heated discussion ensued for about ten minutes, tempers flaring and accusations flying...

"Yes, I can see them, the faint lights. I'm sorry, guys, Carlos was right about the lights. They're there," someone finally admitted.

Carlos handed the rudder over to Eddy and approached Ana, gently trying to help her sit up.

"Come on, I want you to see the lights with us. You're soaked through. I'll change your blouse for this one, it's a little drier," he said softly.

With care, he helped Ana change into the drier blouse.

"Ah, against the waves, you'll just get soaked again," Carlos remarked.

"Don't worry, Carlos, I'm fine," Ana reassured him.

Returning to the helm, they spent about three hours navigating toward the distant lights they had spotted. It felt like an eternity, the lights teasingly close yet seemingly unreachable.

"This boat isn't making any progress, Carlos. What's going on?" Eddy questioned.

"Nothing, kid, it's just how it is. We need to hold on a little longer, that's all," Carlos replied, his tone strained.

"Yes, easy for you to say, Carlos..." Eddy muttered.

"Stand up, this boat is nearly capsizing. There's a strong current; that's why we're not making much headway. I must be cautious," Carlos instructed.

After some time, they finally neared the lights. Eddy spotted something and exclaimed, "There, it looks like a pier, and I see a house too!"

They navigated toward the small dock, and everyone disembarked, except for

Ana, who was too weak to join in the celebration. Holding lanterns, they signaled for assistance.

Carlos returned to the boat and helped Ana ashore. She could barely walk; her legs numb and cold.

Unbeknownst to them, they were trying to confirm their location and seek assistance. Shortly after, a woman and two men emerged from the house and approached them. Despite the language barrier, they attempted to communicate.

"Cuban... water..." someone managed to say.

Two of the locals returned to the house to call the American Coast Guard. Water was brought to them, and photos were taken of the boat and its occupants.

When the ambulance arrived, two of them were taken to the hospital while the other two were escorted to the Coast Guard Center, where they would reunite shortly afterward.

ARRIVAL DATE: MAY 4, 1991

ARRIVAL LOCATION: CABO MARATON, FLORIDA, USA.

St. Petersburg
UNITED STATES
Grand Bahama
Freeport
Miami
BIMINI ISLANDS
Key West
Straits of Florida
Greater Bahama
Andros Island
Cay Sal Bank (THE BAHAMAS)
Havana
Guinchos (THE BAHAM
Matanzas
el Río
Santa Clara
Cienfuegos
CUBA

CHAPTER III
THE EXILE'S REALITY

** The Deception of a Cuban Revolution Veteran**

Seventy-four years have passed, a lifetime of untold tales, my grandfather, a veteran of the Cuban Revolution, now frail, once a figure of strength, now burdened by the weight, of memories and regrets, dreams lost to fate.

Each day merges into the next, a relentless march of time, His existence tinged with sadness, his spirit's climb, reflecting on the years gone by, the sorrows he's known, Longing for a past where freedom's seeds were sown.

I would be happy if I succeeded after so much disappointment to throw back the years that fate holds. Oh, but time does not stop nor does the river twist its course, nor does the dead bird in the jungle return to the empty nest, nor does heaven want me to return hope to my chest.

My Grandpa

And so, I arrived on the shores of Freedom. Since then, I've cherished the liberty I now enjoy, and that my children also share. It wasn't easy to bring my daughter out of Cuba, her parents branded as deserters of that oppressive regime. But thanks to the efforts of Mirtha Colina and the intervention of Florida congresswoman Ileana Ros-Lehtinen, my daughter was able to taste the most precious of human rights: "Freedom".

Upon my arrival, I was directed to the Immigration Base in Miami, where I encountered countless stories of Cuban rafters like me. There, I learned that my journey was just one among many.

I met a young girl who had arrived merely two days before me. She had spent fifteen harrowing days at sea, accompanied by eight others; tragically, most did not survive. They were forced to bid farewell to their loved ones, casting their bodies into the unforgiving depths of the ocean—siblings, spouses, friends.

But these stories are not mine alone to tell; there are countless more like them. That's why I feel compelled to speak out against Castro's regime. Sometimes, I wonder if the world is blind to these atrocities. If only Cubans had the freedom they seek within their own borders, many would never have left. Most exiles would be reunited with their families on the Island today.

When I left my homeland, I never imagined I'd experience true freedom, the ability to voice my thoughts openly. That's why I struggle to comprehend why Castro is revered by some. He is a despicable tyrant, destroying an entire nation, seizing properties unlawfully, and sinking boats filled with defenseless people—children, women, and the elderly—who merely seek freedom. He even shot down planes carrying brave individuals risking their lives to save fellow Cubans in the Straits of Florida.

Yet, I remain perplexed by those who support this tyrant. They must either be blind or unwilling to acknowledge reality. The Cuban people lack the means to overthrow the Castro regime; they don't even have the right to free elections. But they know there are many of us fighting against this dictatorship.

It's been eight years since I left my homeland; I've lost touch with my mother and brother. But I know I'm not alone. However, I'll never return while Cuba remains under this government of lies and tyranny.

Every day, the Cuban people suffer further degradation. Hundreds of political prisoners languish in Cuban jails, simply for demanding the freedom rightfully theirs.

One day, the oppressive regime imposed by the infamous Fidel Castro will crumble. It has been a nightmare for our people over these dreadful forty years. But you should know, the tragedy didn't begin where my story starts. It began on January 1, 1959

*January 1, 1959, Cuban Revolution, establish of the new Cuban government led by Marxist-Leninist and communist Fidel Castro.

What will you do for Freedom?

Cuban Rafters

Is a testimonial book that recovers the memory of the thousands of Cubans who lost their lives in the straits of Florida in search of the long-waited Freedom……

We are deeply grateful to the American people for their immense kindness and for granting us asylum. We also extend our heartfelt thanks to all those with big hearts who have supported us along the way.

Brothers to the Rescue

Tugboat March 13

Rafters at Refugees Key West Center, FL

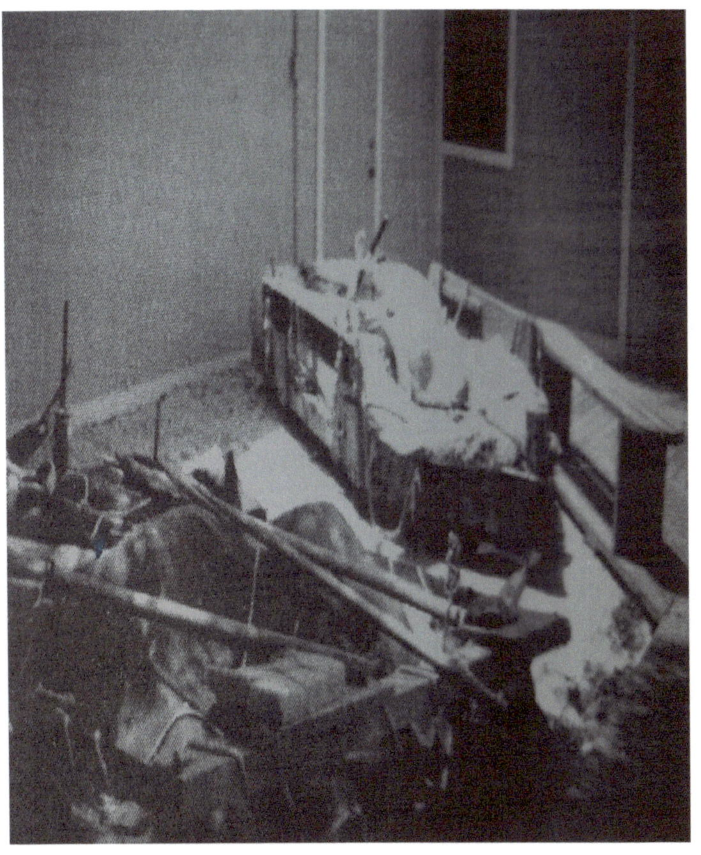

Cuba, 1950's

Cuba today……

Ailema, The Boat to Freedom